VEDANTA
IN
PRACTICE

VEDANTA IN PRACTICE

SWAMI PARAMANANDA

GYAN

Published by

GYAN

Gyan Publishing House
5, Ansari Road
Daryaganj, New Delhi-110002
Phone: 011-47034999, 9811692060
E-mail: books@gyanbooks.com

Distribution Network
gyanbooks.com
India, USA, Canada, UK, Australia

ISBN: 978-93-6433-665-9 (PB)
First Published, 1917

2nd Impression 2024

Printed at: Gyan Press, Delhi.

VEDANTA IN PRACTICE
Author: SWAMI PARAMANANDA

VEDANTA IN PRACTICE

SWÂMI PARAMÂNANDA

VEDANTA IN PRACTICE

BY

SWÂMI PARAMÂNANDA

THE AUTHOR OF
"The Path of Devotion," etc.

NEW YORK
THE BAKER AND TAYLOR COMPANY
MCMIX

This little book is dedicated to the memory of my blessed Master, Swami Vivekananda, whose pure character, unselfish love and teachings of tolerance have tied the East and West in sisterly bonds of love and sympathy.

PREFACE

In giving religious instruction, it is always important to show how principles can be put into practice. People sometimes imagine that the principles are all, and that when one has learned them and can talk glibly about them, nothing further is necessary. This is as great a mistake as to suppose that looking at a well-spread table is all that is needed to satisfy hunger. Unless we not only eat the food, but also digest and assimilate it, so that it becomes part of our bodies, nourishing and preserving them, all the food in the world would be of little use to us.

The aim of these lectures is to show

us how to avail ourselves of the great principles of Vedanta, so that they will become part of our daily lives; to teach us how we can put them into practice and live by them every moment of our existence. When we can thus assimilate them, they will nourish and sustain our spiritual nature, just as food preserves our physical frame. Vedanta is eminently practical, and each of the five lectures is designed to help the reader to put into practice the truth he has learned. They were given in response to the demand for instruction of this character, and they are sent out with the earnest hope that some may be helped by them.

CONTENTS

VEDANTA IN PRACTICE

"Learn this by reverence by enquiry and by humble service. Those men of wisdom who have realized the truth will teach you this Supreme Wisdom.

"Knowing which, thou shalt not again thus fall into error and by which thou shalt see all beings in thyself and also in Me.

"Even if you are the most sinful of the sinful, you will cross over the ocean of sin by the bark of wisdom.

"As kindled fire reduces fuel to ashes, so does the wisdom fire reduce all actions to ashes. Nothing indeed in this world purifies equal to wisdom. He who is perfected by *yoga* (religious practices) finds it in time, *within* himself."

BHAGAVAD GITA IV. 36-38.

I

THE NEED OF SPIRITUAL LIFE

OFTEN it has been asked that something practical in Vedanta teaching should be given—something which can be lived and carried out in our every-day life. This is a very vital point in religion, and without this we cannot expect to be truly spiritual. Of what use is religion, of what use is spirituality, if they have not something to give us more tangible, more substantial, than mere dry words? Frequently we hear people complain of religion and of those who believe in it; they say it is all superstition, intended only for the uneducated and weak-minded. These men are doubtless perfectly sincere in their remarks, because, their vision being limited, they do not see truth behind the claims of religion, and therefore try to deny its existence. Thank God that religious truths do not in the least depend on any such remarks or opinions. If they did not have as their basis something more solid and sublime than we imagine, or perceive, or grasp through our senses, they would not be in existence to-day. For has it not been the special tendency of a certain class of men, in all ages, even from prehistoric times, to endeavor to crush religious truths out of existence? Men of gigantic intellect have often tried to disprove their reality and usefulness. Often great scientists have made bold assertions doubting these truths, because they could not realize them through scientific methods. Many, many waves of antagonism have swept over religion, still it stands firm in its own glory, unshaken and undisturbed. What other proof is necessary to establish its loftiness and extraordinary strength? True religion stands on a pedestal of eternal truth, which no amount of human effort can shake or move. However, it is very interesting to observe that many of these men who at first have risen in opposition, come sooner or later to a realization of its wonderful truth and bow their heads before it. Proof of this is seen in the lives of some great scientists, like Huxley and Tyndall, etc., who, after their lifelong experiences in material science, admitted at the close of their lives that one must give up matter and rise above it, in order to gain knowledge of the spirit. However we may try or struggle, it is certain that spirit guides matter, and will always do so. It cannot be otherwise. Society has always paid its homage to spirituality, but never spirituality to society. This has been the one unique and inevitable law in this world of ours.

Coming back to our point, I must say that religion really teaches the practical side of life. In fact, it is based on realization. What right has a man to say religion is true if he has not seen it and proved it for himself? Similarly, what right has a man to claim it is untrue before he has practised it and tried to realize it? A blind man does not see the sun, and may say that the sun does not shine; but can that really affect the sun, or prove it non-existent? No, it cannot. During a cloudy day the brilliant sun may be hidden and invisible, but can we thereby, in any way, conclude that it does not exist? Exactly in the same way, as long as man's sun of wisdom is covered by the veil of ignorance, he does not see God nor feel the need of a spiritual life. However, nobody can remain forever in that state of unwisdom. Every mistake we make, every experience we gain, whether good or bad, pleasant or unpleasant, always takes us to some higher understanding and realization. But it is very important for spiritual aspirants not to become self-centered and narrow-minded. We all know how limited human knowledge is. One may be very great on his own plane of thought, and another may be as great or greater on an entirely different plane of thought.

Should they, therefore, quarrel and argue—trying to prove that one is right and the other wrong? Both are right, both are true, where is the room for fight or quarrel? Each understands according to his own degree of comprehension. This has been one of the great impediments to spiritual progress, that men entirely lose sight of all things except what they see and feel in their own range of vision. This mistake comes from man's ignorance or extreme egotism, which makes him short-sighted and self-centered. However, this great obstacle is to be overcome through realization. There is no other way out of it. The more ignorant the man, the greater is apt to be his pride of knowledge. We all know this perfectly well. There is no harder task than trying to make an ignorant, egotistical man understand beyond his range of thought. When man is ripened in wisdom his whole nature becomes softened and tender. His whole nature changes, and he becomes broad and sympathetic.

We can study this fact from the lives of all great spiritual men. Their wisdom makes them humble and meek. The wisdom of Socrates made him realize that he knew nothing. Who can really master all of the infinite store of knowledge? The more a man learns, the more he finds before him to learn. There is no limit. Infinite is the ocean of wisdom. The deeper you dive in that ocean, the greater grows your humility. That is the reason we find so much modesty in all the great teachers of mankind. How can they help it, when they see the power of the Almighty One working everywhere in everything? They no longer grovel in the darkness of ignorance, but sing boldly the infinite glory of the Lord. "Thou art one Infinite Being, beyond all human conception, beyond mind and speech." Thus sang the ancient Seers-of-truth, concerning the infinite glory of the Lord. This is what is called true wisdom, knowing the omnipotent power of the invisible force which guides the universe and all that dwells therein, both animate and inanimate. After knowing, through realization, this one and irresistible force, called by different names, as Lord, God, Allah, and so on, how can men help but resign their own wills and say, as did the Nazarene, "Not my will, but Thine, be done"? Not that Jesus alone declared this, but all who attain to this highest state of spiritual wisdom say the same. In all countries and in all ages, Truth is one without a second, and those who realize it also come to the same goal and the same understanding, although we often find a difference in the way of expression or language. This is of little importance; the difference is only in words, and not in the ultimate meaning.

Fools and fanatics do not understand this, and that is why there is so much unnecessary disturbance in the matter of religious opinions. "Why can I not worship my God, my Ideal, by expressing my devotional feelings in my own way without being condemned, criticized or interfered with? Why do I meet so much opposition?" Many ask this question, but it often goes unanswered. Narrow-minded people have only one way of regarding things, and that way is only what they think right. All else is false. Not only do they not want to go beyond the range of their own ideas, but they wish others to accept their views. We have a very beautiful and appropriate illustration in the *Katha-Upanishad:* "Fools dwelling in darkness, wise in their own conceit and puffed up with vain knowledge, go round and round, staggering to and fro, like blind men led by the blind." There are many like this in the world, who, though wrapped in the veil of ignorance, fancy in the pride of their hearts that they know everything. They do not stop there, but try to lead others, and the result is that "the blind, leading the blind, both fall into the ditch."

So when we talk about the impracticability of religion, we must stop for a minute and think, before making such assertions. At present we have become so dependent on matter, and have so lost sight of the spirit that nothing seems practical but bread and butter, and such things as are perceivable and gratifying to the senses. If we weigh all our so-called intellectual arguments against the value of religion, we will see clearly that there is no other reason for our objections, except that we have formed a morbid habit of depending entirely on matter—upon the external and transitory things of this world. But it is a well-known fact that men cannot live on bread alone. Doubtless, food sustains our physical bodies, but it cannot bring any nourishment to the inner life, which is the real self of man—the *Atman*. And sooner or later this need is felt in every human heart. However brutal, diabolical and hard-hearted a man may be; nay, however great his hatred for spiritual truths may be, some day, after going through many different experiences of life, he comes to the conclusion that he cannot live without getting something real, something more substantial than the mere external satisfactions of the world, on which he depended so entirely. This makes him restless. He struggles as if to get some food for his soul. This brings him to a realization of the need of a spiritual life. The value of religion is felt when we come to this point, and not before. Then alone we realize the transitoriness of this world and the necessity of a spiritual life. This shows how we change our views according to our growth and understanding. We cannot make any one spiritual until this need is felt in his heart. The great men of realization know this, and that is the reason they sympathize with those who have not yet awakened to their spiritual necessities. It is through sympathy one can teach, but not through fault-finding. If you want to help anybody, you must come to his level, you must explain things in his language. This is only possible for one who has himself attained spiritual realization.

As I have already said, religion is realization and thoroughly practical. To spiritual men it is even more practical, more real than eating and drinking. There are men who can very easily do away with everything in this world, but find it impossible to live without Divine contemplation. In one pole of existence you will find that men cannot live a day without depending entirely on matter or external surroundings. Similarly you will find, in the other existence, other men to whom it is impossible to live without entirely depending on God and living a spiritual life. This shows that the idea of practicability varies in different stages of life, according to our growth and understanding. If we always bear this in mind, then we can never commit the blunder of denunciation, which comes through short-sightedness or fanaticism.

One great virtue we can all learn from India's spiritual men. They have been very sincere, bold and broad in their assertions. Sometimes it took lives, and even ages to attain to one spiritual truth, but they bore it patiently and went through all prescribed disciplines, hardships and austerities. Even then if they failed they did not find fault with the fundamental teaching, but recognized their own human weaknesses and limitations. This is what is called true wisdom—when we learn to see our own imperfections and limitations. Why should we be so very narrow as to denounce anything, only because we cannot understand it? Our duty is to follow faithfully the spiritual practices with sincerity and purity of heart, and struggle hard till we have realized the truth for ourselves. Nothing else can remove our doubts, nothing else can make us peaceful and happy. Reasoning, talking and studying different scriptures cannot give us happiness, nor supply our inner needs.

Undoubtedly they give some pleasure to intellectual people, but they cannot bring any development of spiritual conceptions. As it has been beautifully expressed by a great Vedantic sage: "The various methods of joining words, the various methods of speaking in beautiful language, the various methods of explaining the diction of the scriptures are only for the disputations and enjoyments of the learned, but they do not lead to freedom." Often we see people carried away by this sort of thing and missing the ultimate goal of human life. Sri Ramakrishna gives a very beautiful parable to this effect. Two friends went to a mango orchard; one of them busied himself in counting the different trees, their branches and leaves, comparing their size and color very carefully. This was undoubtedly very interesting to him. Meanwhile the other went forward, made the gardener his friend and began to enjoy the fruits. Which one of them do you suppose was really the wiser? Certainly the one who enjoyed the fruits. There are people who spend their whole lives in this leaf-counting business, thinking this is the only practical thing in life. And at last they find themselves deceived by the charm of *Mâyâ*. But a few, through proper understanding, avoid this unprofitable labor of leaf-counting and try to acquire the friendship of the owner of this magnificent garden, and thus enjoy the immortal and blissful fruits. They are the best and wisest of all human beings who direct their energies to realizing the Real, distinguishing right from wrong. So we always need right discrimination, in order to live a true spiritual life. Otherwise there is great danger of abusing our powers and energies, and of spending them in wrong directions. But right discrimination saves us from this.

The next thing necessary to have is faith. What is this faith? Often we are told not to have blind faith, not to take anything for granted. That is very true and very rational. We ought to investigate, that is what our reason is for. We must strive hard and find the right path and then follow it faithfully. By faith is meant to trust the scriptures and the words of Seers-of-truth. This is very necessary and helpful in spiritual life. The question may be brought forth, Why should we accept their words before we know their truths ourselves? This is very good as talk, but when we come to practice we find it different. It is hard to realize, and sometimes it takes ages to discover one truth. So it is absolutely necessary to have faith in the words of great prophets and sages who have devoted their whole lives to realizing truth, and to follow their prescribed directions. This can be explained in other words. As a forlorn, thirsty traveler needs the direction of a man who is well acquainted with a strange country and knows where water is to be had, so we, too, need the help of those who can guide us to the "water of life." If we, through our vanity, doubt the words of those true friends who know well all the various intricate ways of spiritual life, we simply miss the opportunity to attain divine wisdom and may die of spiritual thirst. Faith is always helpful and without it spiritual growth becomes impossible. As it is said by Lord Krishna in the Gita: "The ignorant, the faithless and one of doubting Self is ruined. There is neither this world, nor the other, nor happiness for one of doubting mind." Without faith we cannot work properly, and progress is impossible. All great workers possessed wonderful faith in themselves and in the Lord. What can a doubting mind do? It loses all its powers and energies by groping hither and thither in darkness. Another name for doubt is darkness. We doubt much while we are in darkness. So, light the candle of wisdom on the altar of your heart and see the incomparable beauty of your own Self and of the Lord, and learn that these are one and inseparable. Do this boldly and become free from all fear, care and all limited ideas that you are a puny mortal, a slave to disease and death, which arise from doubt of yourself. Or do as Lord Krishna commanded his disciple: "With the sword of wisdom cut asunder this doubt of Self lying in the heart, born of ignorance, and arise." This is the real boldness. Blessed, indeed, are those who can obey such a command to attain freedom. Man, you talk of boldness, this is true boldness which enables you to become the possessor of immortal bliss. This is infinitely greater than all your physical heroic actions, when you can sacrifice all the selfishness and all the vanities of the world, to obey the command of the Lord and live a spiritual life.

II

RIGHT DISCRIMINATION

"Three things are rare and only obtainable through the grace of the Supreme Being: human life, earnest desire for liberation, and the helpful association of the Holy." So it is said by the great illumined sage, Sankara. Why should it be so? Why human life should be considered so great may be questioned. According to the Vedantic conception of creation, this human body is the greatest body in the universe. Man is greater than all animals; nay, than all *Devas* (angels). No other manifestation of life is greater than man. Man alone is in a fit position to attain perfection. Even the

Devas have to come down and attain to perfection through human bodies. The meaning is that, in the lower creation, the animal plane, everything is full of dullness, and thought cannot go farther than the limits of the body. Animals cannot think of any high things. So, also, the *Devas,* who are supposed to live in the heavens, cannot attain to freedom directly. Too much bodily pleasure also ties us to the physical plane and obstructs growth, and high thoughts cannot come. In human society we find the same thing. Those who have too much wealth, or those who are stricken with extreme poverty, are not fit for spiritual attainment: both are great impediments to the development of the soul. It is the middle class who attain wisdom, because here alone we find the forces of mind and body properly adjusted and balanced. This is the reason why human birth is so much esteemed—as the human plane stands between the animal and the angel.

Next is to have the earnest desire or thirst for liberation. How many among us really desire freedom—although we are all human beings? There are few who strongly desire to search for the real, and who realize that all external things are unreal, false. Those who strive earnestly and sincerely to find the way to freedom and succeed in getting the helpful guidance of a true teacher, an illumined soul, are indeed blessed and have accomplished the purpose of human existence. This is the aim and object of human life, although the majority have forgotten it and have taken other things as their ideals. But there comes a moment in every one's life when he cannot but turn toward the truth. He is indeed a true man who strives for liberation, self-mastery, by conquering his lower nature. This human body is a privilege, and those who, after having obtained this great privilege, do not put it to the right use, miss their opportunity.

What makes man greater than the animals? What makes one man greater than another? It is through intelligence that the power of understanding comes. It is through the opening of the faculty of discrimination that one rises higher in thoughts and in wisdom. In the physical plane there is very little opening of this faculty of discrimination. On the intellectual plane it is much more pronounced, but it is not entirely revealed to a man until he has reached the realm of the Spiritual. This discrimination is called, in Sanskrit, *Viveka* and is most important in every step of spiritual life. *Viveka* means discriminating between the real and the unreal, between the true and the false. This world is a great mixture. There are good things as well as bad things; there are beautiful things as well as ugly things; there are beneficial things as well as harmful things; and we are placed in the midst of this turmoil to find our way out of it to that state where there is no duality, but only one existence of Absolute Bliss. So we need this *Viveka* to help us and lead us in the right path.

Without right discrimination we cannot make any progress whatsoever in the spiritual path. Things of the world, beautiful and fascinating to the senses —appearing to be real—often lead us astray when we lack right discrimination. Hard indeed is the path of *Samsâra* (earthly life). Even the keenest human beings are sometimes deceived by the charm of *Mâyâ.* Ignorance is the cause of all our misery and suffering, and ignorance exists because of non-discrimination. When we take the unreal for the real and cling to it, we become disappointed and thus suffer.

We see everything constantly changing around us. The baby becomes the youth, the youth becomes the man who, in his turn, is slowly approaching old age. The strong are weakened by disease, and death comes to all. Yet all are clinging to this life, looking upon this as permanent. What else can be the cause of this delusion, except ignorance and forgetfulness of the true Self? We have identified the immortal Self with this little body which is bound to fall. "Ignorance is taking that which is non-eternal, impure and non-Self, for the Eternal, pure, blissful *Atman* (Self)."

Our present conception of the Self is nothing beyond the body. But the body cannot be the Self. The body can never become unchangeable or eternal. Everything that has a beginning must necessarily have an end. It cannot be otherwise. The body comes and goes, being a combination of matter, but the Spirit remains always—unchangeable and eternal.

Once, Indra, the head of the gods, and Virochana, the head of the demons, went to learn about the Self from a great sage. They both studied with him for a long time. Then, one day, their master declared, "Thou art that. Thou thyself art that Self which thou art seeking." Both of them were at first pleased, and thought they had accomplished everything. They returned to their homes and gave the message to the people. The demon, having naturally a clouded and ignorant nature, could not understand the real meaning of the words of the sage, but took them literally, and thought his body was the Self. So he declared to his people, "Make the body well and strong by taking good food and exercise. Be happy. None is greater than ourselves. We are *Brahman*." Thus he remained contented, and inquired no further.

But the god had a much finer nature, and he at once began to think:

"The meaning of our master's words cannot be that the Self is this body. How can this body be the Self while it is so ephemeral, changeable and dependent on matter? The Self does not change at all." So he returned to the sage and asked, "Sir, did you mean that this body is the Self? I see that the body changes constantly and dies, while the Self is unchangeable and immortal." The sage replied, calmly, "Thou art that Self. Find it out thyself."

Then Indra thought perhaps the vital forces were the Self. But soon he found that they became weak if he did not give them proper nourishment. So he came back to the sage to find if he meant the vital forces. But the sage answered in the same way. Then Indra thought it must be the mind, but soon he discovered that the mind could not be the Self, as it is sometimes happy and at other times unhappy. Thus, through constant search, patience and right discrimination, and through the help of the sage, the god attained Self-knowledge — the Self which is neither body nor mind, but beyond both, "whom the sword cannot cut, whom fire cannot burn, whom water cannot melt, and air cannot dry. Birthless, deathless, One, omniscient and all-pervading." The god, through proper discrimination, reached the goal, while the poor, ignorant demon missed it on account of his fondness for the body and bodily pleasures.

We need not go far to find out the significance of this story. You will excuse me if I say that in human society we find a good many demons whose thoughts do not go beyond the limits of the body and are perfectly satisfied with sense pleasures. But there are a few gods, too, who can differentiate through discrimination the real from the unreal, and release the soul from the bondage of *Mâyâ*. We can all become like gods if we only use this power properly, and manifest Divinity within ourselves. Similarly we can degrade ourselves to the animal plane if we do not use it properly. Our progression or retrogression depends entirely upon ourselves, on our every thought and action. The Lord has given us the power of discrimination, and if we use it we can rise higher—but if we neglect it and are led away by our momentary impulses, then we obstruct our growth and remain almost as ignorant as animals. "The tendencies of eating, sleeping, fear and sense enjoyments are common to both human beings and animals. The former excel the brutes in knowledge and understanding. But those who lack in knowledge can be classified with animals."

Some may think this is put in a rather exaggerated form, but it is not so. On the contrary, much truth can be found in it if properly analyzed.

There are three planes of existence in this universe. The first is the physical or material, the manifestation of which is shown obviously in animal life. The thoughts in this plane of existence cannot go beyond the body and senses, and the mind naturally dwells in that circle. The second is the plane of intellect where human beings are supposed to stand. The manifestation of intellect is especially seen in our great scientists and mechanicians who, through their many researches and inventions, have helped mankind. The tendency of intellect is to overcome all physical limitations and to give man more power over himself and nature in general. This is undoubtedly higher than the physical plane, but still higher is a plane which is known as the spiritual plane. This stands entirely beyond the body and mind. No amount of physical strength or intellectual keenness can bring us to this plane. This is the state in which we experience supernatural powers, which neither the senses nor the intellect can bring to us.

These three planes of existence are the manifestation of *Sattva, Rajas* and *Tamas,* as they are called in Sanskrit. These three are the principal elements out of which all living forms are manufactured. Our bodies are more or less the combination of these three. *Tamas* is the lowest, as represented by animals. The nature of *Tamas* is darkness and dullness, and when these predominate in man he becomes stupid and inactive. His mind is filled with evil propensities, and he fails to distinguish between right and wrong. This class of men is very little removed from the animals, because they do not possess the power of proper judgment, and their whole thought and action are centralized in their bodies. They often injure others to fulfil their selfish desires. But the intellect helps us to uplift ourselves above this dull, material plane. Through the help of intellect we become active and ambitious for happiness. This is the nature of *Rajas.* Through *Rajas* we become immensely active, and thus overcome all dullness. In this way, through the power of reasoning, we progress much. But soon we find that the human intellect falls back after reaching a certain point. Here man struggles hard to penetrate the wall which stands between him and the Unknown. However, through the earnest struggle of the soul, a channel is opened which gives him the power to see inner things. This is the state of *Sattva,* where man is neither satisfied by fulfilling the physical desires nor contented to remain within the limits of the intellect, but stands steadily keeping the balance of both. In this state alone he can rightly discriminate.

Sattva gives the equilibrium and enables us to think and act rightly.

According to the manifestation of these three qualities—*Sattva, Rajas* and *Tamas*—we see the differences in human beings. The man who possesses the quality of goodness, in him alone we see true fearlessness, uprightness, purity, truthfulness, forgiveness and the absence of all anger and passion. He alone becomes peaceful and happy through his self-control. There is no other way to get peace. The man who follows the path of *Rajas* (or the quality of passion) never finds any peace or rest, as there is no limit to human desires. The more we gratify them, the stronger they become. It is just like adding fuel to the fire—we but make the flame stronger.

How can any man expect to find

peace and happiness when he is overpowered by *Tamas* or the darkness of ignorance? Through our experience we come to the conclusion that we must learn how to control our lower natures and manifest goodness, by which means alone we can hope to attain perfection. Thus discrimination becomes our true friend on the spiritual path by showing us the right way and saving us from errors.

Now the question is, how to cultivate this quality of *Sattva?* "By practice and non-attachment it is attained." Of course there are some suggestions regarding food. By living on pure food one can change his body and gain *Sattva* elements. It is true that one can be helped by proper food and drink.

There are three causes which make

food impure. The nature of the food itself, such as onions, garlic, etc.; when it is polluted by any foreign substance, such as hair, dirt, etc.; and, thirdly, when it is touched by an impure person.

By avoiding these three, we can undoubtedly gain strength and goodness, but one thing we must always remember, and that is that all external observances are only secondary. The real purity is internal, and only obtainable through the constant practice of unselfishness and chastity. When we lack discrimination, there is great danger of our falling into fanaticism—that most deadly of all foes to progress. However, if we keep the goal constantly before our eyes and in our hearts, then we can safely overcome all obstacles that lie in our way.

All outer observances regarding cleanliness, food, etc., are intended only as helps toward our spiritual development, and should not be mistaken for the goal itself. So we must be ever watchful, and guard ourselves from attaching undue importance to any merely external actions. Everything in this world has its legitimate use and also can easily be abused. So we need to discriminate in every step, in order to use our energies in the right direction. The following will illustrate this: "Once upon a time there lived a yogi, a holy man, who practised daily at certain hours. During this time he was much disturbed by a cat, so in order to have unbroken meditation he confined the animal in the next room. This went on for a long time, until finally he passed away, leaving behind him a disciple. Now, the disciple sincerely tried to imitate his master in every way. With that end in view, he spent much of his time trying to get hold of a cat, thinking that this animal had been an essential part of his master's meditation!"

We often make a similar blunder, and, mistaking the non-essential for the essential, waste our forces in vain.

Most of our religious disharmonies are the direct result of these unassimilated ideas. Great souls do things with a certain purpose in view, and their followers, not understanding the proper spirit of their actions, misinterpret them, often to their own hindrance. Rituals and ceremonies should not be our main object in worship, but should be regarded merely as helps toward the goal. If we forget, and make them cur first and foremost consideration, then we are easily misled, and our growth is retarded. Therefore, let us then seek sincerely and watch carefully; always working steadily, with perseverance, faith and discrimination and through the grace of the Lord we shall attain salvation.

III

BUILDING OF CHARACTER

EVERYTHING in this world is transitory, is fleeting. From the highest manifestation of human life to the lowest worm, all are destined to perish. No man was ever born who could stop his body from changing constantly. Body is the name of a series of changes. What remains, then, but character? Time swallows up everything except character; this is the only thing it cannot touch.

If we look back and study the history of mankind, we find that, no matter how hard the struggle may have been to live here forever, in the end all have been conquered by death. Emperors and kings have striven to build up something permanent, something imperishable, but in vain. Look at the mighty Roman Empire, look at the wonderful Greek civilization, where are they? The one has crumbled into dust, the other lies in ruins. And what has outlived them? The message of Jesus Christ, the son of a carpenter, and that of the beggar Buddha. They are still ruling the universe. Mysterious are the ways of the Lord. Those who wanted to live have died; those who were willing to die have continued to live. Christ, who freely gave up His life, lives eternally. Buddha, who renounced a whole kingdom, rules over half the world.

Why did these great Teachers renounce? Because they found that everything that is a combination of matter is destined to perish; and they sought something more permanent. When Christ was tempted by the devil, He cast aside the world because He well knew its hollowness and that it could never bring real happiness. So Buddha resisted the temptations of Mâra, because he had realized that this world could bring only sorrow in the end. Both of these great Souls valued character more than all else, and devoted all their attention to that. They renounced, or threw aside, all else, knowing that everything was transitory, that character alone would live.

One obvious thing in all spiritual characters is, that they especially tend toward renunciation, as without it spiritual growth is impossible. This idea of renunciation is often misunderstood, and the majority of human beings are even horrified by the mere mention of it. Yet we know that it forms the very foundation of spiritual life, and we see how all great men drew their inspiration and strength from this source. Show me one great spiritual character who did not sacrifice all selfishness and go through supreme renunciation. "You cannot serve both God and mammon." There is a great deal of meaning in this simple saying of the Lord. It is not as easy as we imagine it to be; we cannot grasp the true meaning of this saying as long as our hearts are weak and impure. What makes us weak and impure? Dependence on matter and forgetfulness of the glorious spirit within; the more you love the world, with all its vanities, and depend on it, the weaker you become in internal strength.

God is the source of all our strength and inspiration, but when we forget Him, through the charm of matter, we become spiritually blind. The one is blinding, while the other is sight-giving—so both cannot co-exist. You cannot have sincere love for God in your heart and at the same time fondness for worldly enjoyments. It is impossible; it is inharmonious—as darkness and light. One must exist at a time. Thus the sages have declared boldly the thought of renunciation: Give up! Give up the world and love God, the Supreme Goal from whom we have come into existence, in whom we live and move and have our being. Do not forget Him, do not neglect to serve Him. Love Him and serve Him and let all else go. This is the watchword of all religions and religious teachers.

This love for God is the object and aim of renunciation.

There is no violence or hard-heartedness necessary in renunciation. It is a natural growth of the heart. When we love God with our whole heart and soul then there is no room for anything else, and renunciation becomes easy.

One thing worthy of mention in this connection is, that renunciation does not necessarily mean running away from one's own home, friends and relatives, or being cruel to them. One can acquire love for God at home by practising non-attachment and unselfishness. The question may be asked, What do we gain by renunciation? Our best reward, our greatest good is to love God above all external things and to gain knowledge of the Supreme. So we see that renunciation is one of the most important factors in the building of character.

What is character? Every act or thought leaves an impression on the mind. All these impressions taken together make up the character. When a large number of similar impressions are left on the mind, they unite and become a habit. It is truly said that "habit is second nature." Indeed, Swami Vivekananda often remarked that it was all the nature we had. What we are to-day is the result of our past. This gives us great consolation and hope, because if what we do is only habit, then we can make or unmake it through our thoughts and deeds.

There are two planes in this universe where our minds dwell. The *Sat*—the real, the permanently existent—and the

Asat—the unreal, the fleeting, the non-existent.

One's standard of good and evil proceeds from these. Anything that is a combination of matter is *Asat,* is fleeting and changeable; when we cling ignorantly to such transitory things to gratify our momentary impulses, we become *Asat,* and it is such unsteady characters which we call bad or evil.

As, however, any one who is bad has become so through habit, through holding his mind on the plane of evil, so he can overcome this tendency by learning to hold his mind on the plane of good, by cultivating a good habit of thought. At first it will be difficult for him, and he will have to struggle hard, but if he persistently looks only for the good everywhere, then, in the end, he is sure to conquer. This is undoubtedly a very difficult task and, however we may try, we are bound to sometimes come in contact with evil; especially is this true for those of us who live in the world, as we cannot very well avoid associating with various classes of people.

What are we to do then? How are we to overcome this difficulty? Patanjali's advice is helpful: "Friendship, mercy, gladness, indifference being thought of in regard to subjects, happy, unhappy, good and evil, respectively, pacify the mind." This is the real secret. It is evident that we cannot entirely avoid evil, but we can counteract and remedy it by holding these four sorts of ideas regarding all things that come before us. We must hold the feeling of friendship toward all, and be merciful to those who are in misery.

When others are happy we should feel happy, too, and to the wicked and evil-minded we must be indifferent. If the subject is good, we must be friendly toward it, because true friendship is only possible and desirable with good and sincere people. You cannot give a friendly embrace to a tiger or a snake; the wisest thing is to avoid them.

Then, if the subject of thought is miserable, we must be merciful toward it. When we see anybody suffer, we must try to remove his misery with a feeling of love and sympathy.

This we must do with unselfishness and non-attachment toward the fruits of our actions. Whether the one whom you help is grateful or otherwise, matters not. Whenever you have the opportunity of helping any one, you must bear in mind that it is for your good, for your own salvation. It is a privilege to serve God in the form of the miserable, and thus build our characters and manifest Divinity.

Next is gladness: we must be glad when others are happy. When any one becomes prosperous, victorious and successful, we must be happy to see him happy.

Instead of entertaining the feeling of jealousy or hatred, we must rejoice in the joy of others. There is no peace or happiness in that heart which cannot stand the good fortune of others.

The last and most difficult precept is to be indifferent to evil subjects. This is hard, because it needs immense self-control to balance the mind and discriminate rightly. The feelings of both love and hatred are natural, but indifference is very difficult to practise. We can love good, but we cannot love evil, however we may talk of loving all. There naturally rises the opposite, hatred, in our hearts. For instance, if a man does evil to us, we at once become disturbed, and react by wanting to injure him. But thereby we gain nothing; we only lose our strength and energy. Every time we get angry or try to counteract evil by hatred we weaken ourselves and obstruct our spiritual growth. So one who possesses the power of discrimination and self-control can alone overcome this difficulty by neither establishing friendship nor animosity with the evil object.

While we hold our minds on the physical plane, we have become weak on the spiritual plane. To regain our spiritual strength we must withdraw our minds from the plane of matter. A great help to this is the company of the holy. Even a moment's association with great men will help us to cross over the ocean of worldliness. Who are great men? Those who are unselfish, all-loving and who remain unmoved under praise or blame, who live in this world not to gain anything for themselves, but to serve and help mankind for love's sake. When we come in contact with such lofty souls, a deep impression is made on our minds and this will gradually change the whole character. The very same man who was wicked may now become a saint. But, although the company of holy men may do much to purify us and change our natures, character is, after all, what we form ourselves by our own habits of thought and by our own deeds. We alone are responsible for our characters. If we are now bad, we can change and become good. It all depends upon ourselves. As long, however, as we remain on the dual plane—on the plane of good and bad—there is danger of falling back. We must, therefore, go beyond both, and reach a state where our characters become perfect. Then neither good nor bad can any longer have an effect upon them; they remain untouched by either. This is the only thing that is regarded as permanent in this transitory world. But until we have reached this state we are not free from danger. Thus a man who lives in solitude and tries to form his character may appear to be perfect, as long as he does not come into evil association, but he cannot be judged until he is seen in the midst of evil. That is the test. A perfect character is one who can go through good and bad unmoved. As it has been beautifully expressed by Emerson, "It is easy in the world to live after the world's opinion; it is easy in solitude to live after our own; but the great man is he who, in the midst of the crowd, keeps with perfect sweetness the independence of solitude." This is the exact definition of a perfect man who is the same under all circumstances.

We need both good and evil to form the perfect character, and the hard blows, which we call evil, often help us more than the good. If we look at the lives of great men, they seem to have gained most from blows—from adversity. Good is necessary, too, but we must especially try to be steady when we come in contact with evil. These great men first overcame evil by practising the good, and then they rose still higher, where they could not be touched by either good or evil—where neither moved them.

Such a character was Suka, who was the son of a great sage and born perfect. At an early age the father sent him to the court of King Janaka, to learn. In order to test him, the king gave certain instructions beforehand to his courtiers, and when the boy arrived at the gate of the palace he was allowed to sit there three days and three nights without being noticed even by the guards of the palace. Then high officials came and received him with royal honor. Still his face did not change; he remained unmoved. When at last he was led before the king, the king gave him a cup of milk, full to the brim, and told him to carry it seven times around the hall without spilling a drop. In the midst of music and dancing the boy walked seven times around the hall with the same calm face without spilling one drop of the milk. Then the king said to him, "You have nothing more to learn. You have known the Truth—go home to your father."

The only true help that you can render to mankind is when, by your very character, you teach others. Then you do good by your every word, your every movement. When, for instance, you remain steady under all conditions of good and evil, those around you learn the value of steadiness and begin to try to practise it themselves.

Thus, by the example of your character, your whole life becomes a lesson to others. This reminds me of a very beautiful and appropriate saying we have in one of our Vedanta Scriptures:

Under a banyan-tree a young illumined spiritual teacher and an old gray-haired disciple were seated. The disciple's mind was full of doubts, of ignorance, and he questioned—but the teacher ever kept silence, and the disciple's doubts were gradually dispelled. Such is the force of character. It speaks louder than language. Its power is wonderfully effective—more than anything else in this universe.

Purity has been the foundation of all truly great characters. If you build a house on the sand, it is sure to tumble down; so, if we build our characters on anything but purity, they will not stand. Impurity is a mixture; purity is one without a second. Mixed thoughts are seeing many; pure thought is when you see only One. When you think of any one's evil side, you yourself take that evil; just as when you meditate on a saint, you gain saintliness. What you think, you become. When we realize how much we lose by dwelling on the plane of evil we grow watchful and hold the mind only on the plane of good, and see in everything the All-pervading God. If we wish to save ourselves, we shall have to struggle hard, we shall have to regain, inch by inch, what we have lost by dwelling on the evil in the world. But it may be said, every one has mixed feelings — sometimes good, sometimes bad. How can we get out of this state? By using the power of discrimination, by constantly training the mind to distinguish the right from the wrong, and to seek only the good. This is the practical life. Building of character is the only true practice of Yoga, and it is the only way we can really help humanity. Christ helped the world by His character. It is not that He turned this earth into a heaven. That is not possible. There was just as much evil in the world after He came as before, but by His example He is helping each individual soul to overcome its limitations and to strive toward perfection.

Neither Christ nor Buddha, or any other prophet, claimed to be exceptions. On the contrary, they preached that all can become like them. We can all become perfect characters. But only when we build our characters on the firm foundations of purity, unselfishness, and non-attachment will they be immovable, and become a blessing to all mankind.

POWER OF CONCENTRATION

When the subdued mind rests in the Self alone, without longing for the objects of desire, that man is said to be a *yogi* (saint).

As the flame of a lamp placed in a windless spot does not flicker, so the heart of the *yogi* of subdued mind remains steadfast in meditation and wavers not.—*Bhagavad-Gita* 6:18, 19.

IV

POWER OF CONCENTRATION

WISDOM is the goal of human existence. Even men of the lowest intelligence want to know the secret of things; because knowledge alone can bring peace and happiness to our souls. Ignorance is the main source of all misery and none really enjoys being in that state. Why do we find so many ignorant, irresponsible people around us, then, if all are eager for wisdom? Because, although the desire for wisdom is the natural instinct in every human heart, but few possess the power of acquiring it. A man who is inactive, stupid and full of ignorance has every desire to be all-knowing, only he does not want to work to gain knowledge. There are others who are capable of work, and are immensely active, but who do not know the secret of work, and only exhaust their energies in wrong directions. The door of knowledge is ready to open to every one of us if we only know how to knock at it properly.

There is only one way to knowledge and wisdom, and that is through the power of concentration. Without this power nobody can accomplish anything in this world. The students who can concentrate their minds fully on their books are the best students. With the least effort they accomplish the most. The scientist, in his laboratory, concentrates all the energies of his mind in one direction, and thus discovers the secrets of Nature. So does the astronomer fix his mind, through his telescope, on sun, moon, planets, etc., and they give up their secrets to him. He is a good musician who can concentrate his mind on his music. So, also, with artists and everybody else. This is the only road to knowledge. The more we can concentrate our minds on the subject of our study, the more rapidly the knowledge of that subject is revealed to us. Now let us see how to acquire this power of concentration, as all our wisdom is based on this, especially spiritual wisdom. All the different practices of yoga are entirely based on concentration.

Patanjali, in his *Yoga Aphorisms,* defines yoga as "restraining the 'mind-stuff' from taking various forms." This is only possible through the power of concentration. What is the present state of our minds? If we properly analyze, we shall find that they take innumerable forms. Sometimes one's mind is happy, again unhappy; sometimes angry, and again quiet, etc. It is always restless. We are all sitting here just now. If we are a little careless, and let the mind run, it will perhaps travel thousands of miles away this minute, and will begin dreaming of various impressions of the past which will make it accordingly happy or unhappy. This is precisely the condition of our minds.

Among those of you who have read Swami Vivekananda's celebrated book on *Râja Yoga,* some perhaps remember how the mind is compared to a maddened monkey. "There was a monkey, restless by his own nature, as all monkeys are. As if that were not enough, some one made him drink freely of wine, so that he became still more restless. Then a scorpion stung him. When a man is stung by a scorpion he jumps about for a whole day, so the poor monkey found his condition worse than ever. To complete his misery, a demon entered into him. What language can describe the uncontrollable restlessness of that monkey? The human mind is like that monkey, incessantly active by its own nature; then it becomes drunk with the wine of desire, thus increasing its turbulence. After desire takes possession, comes the sting of the scorpion of jealousy of others whose desires meet with fulfilment; and, last of all, the demon of pride takes possession of the mind, making it think itself of all importance." Such is the general condition of the mind. How hard it is to control such a mind! Nobody can do this for us. We can get many helpful suggestions from our teachers, but we can achieve self-mastery only through our own efforts. It must be our own work.

Arjuna, the disciple, after listening to the wonderful teaching of the *Gita* from his master, Krishna, said, "This yoga of equanimity taught by thee, I see not its steady continuance, because of the restlessness of my mind." To that, the blessed Lord replied: "Doubtless, O Mighty-Armed, the mind is restless and hard to restrain, yet by constant practice and dispassion it is subdued." There is no other way. We ourselves must accomplish the work of subduing the mind by our perseverance and unfailing practice. *Yogis,* or spiritual men, through their careful study, have found out all the various intricate tendencies of the mind and body and also how one can subdue them through different practices of concentration, and so attain absolute self-mastery.

Our mind manifests itself in various forms: *Kshipta, Mudha, Vikshipta* and *Ekâgra. Kshipta* means scattered. We often find our mind in this stage when our thoughts are various and the mind jumps from one thing to another. This is a state of activity, and the mind runs after sense pleasures. But no real peace or happiness can be found while it is in this scattered state. The nature of the second is dullness, inactivity, and one becomes indiscriminative and injures others. Next is *Vikshipta,* or the weakening state of mind. In this state we struggle to centralize the mind, but often without success. When we do not find satisfaction, either in the scattered or dull state of mind, then we begin to struggle for some higher form. If one perseveres, one reaches the state of *Ekâgra,* the concentrated or one-pointed mind. Only when the mind arrives at this state do we attain to superconsciousness and become free forever. The first three states are not fitted to bring spiritual realization. But in the last stage, through the power of concentration, we can collect all our mental and physical energies, and direct them toward the highest realization.

When the mind is not concentrated, it is weak and we cannot accomplish anything with it. Our mind in one of the first three states is like thin fibres, which are scattered and separated one from the other; it cannot stand any pressure, but breaks easily. But through the power of concentration, when we can collect it into one mass, then we are able to resist all distractions, even as the twisted fibres can resist the strength of an elephant.

The value of concentration is unquestionable. It helps every one in every stage of life. But the greatest man is he who can concentrate his mind on the Supreme Reality, as "we become exactly what we think." Intense thought forms our external and internal nature. This we can often see in the case of devoted husband and wife; they become like each other in their manners; nay, even in their appearance. This fact is very obviously shown in the life of Saint Francis of Assisi, who by constantly concentrating his mind on Jesus the Christ became

Christlike. It is even said his external figure became transformed and showed the marks of the stigmata. Such is the power of concentration that it can change the whole nature of a man. By concentrating our minds on a pure, holy being we become holy. Similarly, when we turn our thoughts to material objects, we become materialistic, and we may accomplish much on that plane.

It is comparatively easy to concentrate our minds on external objects, but it is very hard to turn our thoughts on things within. Very few have the patience or courage to do it. We must take some tangible object on which to concentrate, and then go on practising till we have fully subdued all other thoughts but that one. For instance, take the thought of unselfishness, or purity. Fill your whole being with that one thought, think of nothing but that, dream of nothing but that, and feel nothing but that, then you will eventually become pure and unselfish. At first your thoughts will rise in opposition. But every time you attempt to subdue them you shall find yourself stronger, and gradually, through constant practice, you will conquer them fully. Real yoga practice is when we try to collect our thoughts from all sources, make them one, and connect them with our Inner Self. Yoga means this union with the Supreme Self which destroys all ignorance. We cannot feel this union, or have the vision of the Self, until our mind is wholly subdued and, like the surface of a lake, is perfectly calm and quiet. As long as there are ripples, in the form of innumerable desires, we cannot see the bottom, where the *Atman* dwells. So our duty is to practise with patience and perseverance until we have succeeded in making our mind one-pointed and have subdued all mixed and wandering thoughts.

This is not the work of a day, but may take years; nay, lives. Progress, however, depends entirely upon our earnestness. There are degrees of earnestness, and our success varies accordingly, as is shown by different temperaments. Some are exceedingly slow in their nature, and do not have any power of determination or perseverance; while others are wonderfully energetic and ready to give up even their lives in their attempts. Sri Ramakrishna gives a parable, to this effect, of two peasants who were working in their fields to bring water. The wife of one came and asked her husband to leave the work until the next day. As it was late, the man, after a little hesitation, left his work. The wife of the other came and urged him and scolded him, but the man was determined to finish his work. At last, after a whole day's toil, he was able to bring the water into his field and could take his rest in peace, knowing his task had been accomplished. There are many among us who lack in steadfastness and discrimination, and simply waste their energies by jumping from one thing to another without any success. No matter what path we may follow, we must learn to be steady and faithful; without this, no knowledge is obtainable. We never lose this power after once acquiring it, and we can utilize this force in every way. When we succeed in concentrating our minds, then meditation comes naturally. "There is no wisdom to the unsteady, and no meditation to the unwise, and to the unmeditative no peace; to the peaceless how can there be happiness?"

What is meditation? Meditation is a constant remembrance of the object we meditate upon. In other words, it is illustrated as "an unbroken stream of oil poured from one vessel to another." When we attain to this kind of remembrance in relation to the Supreme Being, then all the bonds of the heart break, and it becomes illuminated by the presence of the Self. Through meditation we feel the nearness of Divinity. There is no other way to reach Him. No external power can give us the vision of God. Because He is the nearest of all friends, nearest of anything that we can perceive. "He is greater than the greatest, smaller than the smallest, and He dwells in the core of every heart." As long as we try to see Him outside of us, we never find Him, all our struggles are in vain. But when, by experience, we find it impossible to see Him outside of us, then we turn our thoughts inside and become meditative.

There are two forces—centrifugal and centripetal. The tendency of one is to drive us toward all external objects, and the tendency of the other is to draw us within. When, through the power of concentration, we can subdue all the various disturbing thoughts and desires, then we shall get the vision of the Supreme Self seated on the altar of our hearts. Then alone all crookedness will be straightened out and all doubts about the Self will vanish forever. We shall be supremely blissful, knowing that we and the Father are one.

V

SELF-REALIZATION

REALIZATION is the watchword of all religions. If there is a God, or a Supreme Self, we must see It, we must realize It. Otherwise these theories about the existence of God and the soul have very little value; if we cannot put them on a practical basis and realize the truth of them, they remain for us but mere words. This realization is the only thing that can bring satisfaction to us. No amount of theory can ever satisfy our minds unless we can see the reality of things for ourselves. The various methods of joining words, the various methods of speaking in beautiful language, and having the skilfulness of expounding the Scriptures cleverly are only for the enjoyment of the learned, but they never lead to spiritual realization, nor can they ever bring freedom. What use is there in studying scriptures if we thereby gain no spiritual wisdom? Studying means to get the directions which lead to the ultimate goal, and when we forget that, we do not gain any profit whatsoever, though we may spend our whole life in reading all the scriptures of the world. We have a very beautiful saying, in this wise: "As a donkey carries loads of sandal-wood on his back, only feeling the weight of the burden without getting the benefit of the sweet perfume, so it is with those who study innumerable scriptures without knowing the essence—the truth—of them; their labor is like that of the donkey carrying the load of wood." What I mean is, that our aim and object should be realization, and not to remain satisfied with a network of words.

There is a great deal of difference between a philosopher, a man of book-learning, and a Seer-of-truth, a man of realization. The philosopher may have studied all the Vedas, and other scriptures, and may be able to quote long passages from them; but the Seer-of-truth knows, because he has seen. The first merely repeats what he has learned; the second says, "Yes, I *know!*" Thus his words are bold. Experience is the real and only way of acquiring strength. Real strength comes through realization; when a man has seen God he can declare with conviction that there is a God. When we have seen a thing, no matter how much people may deny the existence of that thing, we can still stand up boldly and declare, "I know it exists."

We hear and study about the immortal nature of our soul, yet we are all the time afraid of dying. Why is that? Because we have no conception of our real nature, we have no realization of the Self, the real man. In fact we have no idea what Soul means; our knowledge is limited to this material body, and if we try to form any idea of ourselves we only do it through this limited body, which is subject to constant changes. So, however we may study, and however we may talk about the immortal nature of our Self; nay, however we may repeat *Soham* (I am He), and other sacred words, all this carries very little weight and strength without the realization of the ultimate meaning of these things. In India parrots are trained to repeat holy names, and as long as they are unmolested they will repeat them; but no sooner does a cat come after them than they give their natural cry, forgetting all about the names they have been taught. Similarly, people repeat the words of the scriptures without comprehending their meaning, and that is why, when trouble comes, they are so miserable, so weak, so much in fear of death.

But when we realize the Self, when we perceive It, as we perceive the existence of those around us, then we can no longer doubt. Then fear of death or of disease will no longer exist. Nature has no influence on the Supreme Self of man, which is in reality one and the same with God, so Self-realization and God-vision are not two different things. Man is the expression of God, and God is the reality of man. Real man and God are inseparable. There is only one reality in this universe, whom the devotee worships as a personal god, and a *Jnâni,* or wise man, as his own Self. The difference is only in names and methods of reaching the goal, but when the goal is reached, both come to the same understanding, that there is but One by Whom everything is pervaded. "This *Atman* is not to be realized by the intellect, nor by words, nor by hearing from many sources; but by him by whom this *Atman* is beloved, by him alone is the *Atman* realized." The thing necessary for us is to feel intense love in our hearts for this *Atman,* or God; otherwise He is not attainable. There is no other way that man can reach unto God, except through love—love always unites. This love for God comes unto those blessed beings who are pure in heart, from whom all attachment for unreal things, all selfish desires have vanished. This purity of heart and love for God are the sum and substance of all religious teachings.

We may spend all our lives struggling in search of truth, in temples, in churches and in books; but without understanding the significance of these fundamental teachings all these efforts will be in vain. Religion is practical, and those who observe the practical side of it realize the truth. You may not know how to read a single book, but if you have known the truth which is behind them you are much better off than the so-called philosopher who may speak in beautiful language, but who has no realization whatsoever. It is a dangerous thing to hear the truth from one who has not realized, for he will only bring confusion in the mind; but one who has realized will teach without uttering many words. As Swami Vivekananda says in one of his lectures, that he who has something to give, gives in most simple language, but one who has nothing to give he sometimes writes two volumes to expound one word. So, you see that we gain nothing when we come in contact with such people; they only confuse our brains.

He who has attained illumination does not need to use many words. His life itself is an answer to all questions —for the sun of wisdom always shines in his heart. This makes one bold; before this strength all other strength is insignificant. When Alexander the Great was in India he met a sage with whose wisdom he was so deeply impressed that he wished to carry him back to Greece, but the sage refused to go. The king offered him wealth and honor; still he refused. Then, at last growing angry, the king said: "If you do not come, I will kill you!" At this the sage smiled, and replied: "King, you never said anything more foolish. You cannot kill me—me whom the sword cannot pierce, whom the fire cannot burn, whom water cannot melt, and air cannot dry. I am the eternal, indestructible soul!" Such strength comes when we attain to Self-realization; then we never depend on anything or anybody, and we become absolutely fearless. No matter how we struggle to find rest, we learn that unless we get peace within ourselves we cannot get it elsewhere.

But it is very hard for those who identify themselves with the body and have too much attachment for sense-pleasures to realize the Self which is beyond all limitation. You remember the story how two seekers after Truth went to a saint to learn about the Self. The saint gave the same teaching to both: "*Tat twam asi* [Thou art That] —the Lord does not exist apart from you; find Him out yourself within yourself." The one, owing to his density and fondness for the body, understood the saying of the saint to mean that his material body was the Self; but the other was finer in nature, and through his earnestness and sincere inquiry came to realize the Self which is beyond body, mind, senses and all human limitations. The thing necessary for us is to always have right discrimination and non-attachment; too much attachment and fondness for the body create bondage and obstruct our spiritual growth. At the same time, those who neglect to take proper care of their bodies retard their spiritual growth and may even make it impossible, as is seen in some individual cases, where the body is broken down by practising too much asceticism. This body should be regarded as an instrument through help of which we are to work out our salvation. For that reason we must take all necessary care of our body to keep it well and strong, without thinking it all in all. The human body is compared to a *Vina* (string instrument) which produces beautiful music if properly tuned. In order to tune properly we need to use moderation; if we put too much pressure on the strings, they give way; and if we use no pressure at all, no music is produced. Here, if we use discrimination, we can save ourselves from being radical materialists or extreme ascetics. Our aim and object are neither the body nor bodily enjoyment, but to gain that knowledge of the Self which will bring us absolute freedom.

We try to get pleasure in this world, but nothing can give that, unless one finds it within his own self. That which is consciousness in this world is the Self, and in That alone we find all our happiness and bliss. Who cares for the material body? We all love the Self, no matter whether we know it or not.

We all love that consciousness which is the Self of man. As long as that consciousness dwells in the body, we care for that body, but the moment the spirit leaves, we no longer care for the empty shell. We may not recognize this fact, for reason of our weakness born of living on the material plane. We follow the regular process of physical life, and we train our children also to do the same; the young are taught to study a little, later to earn money, then to marry, have pleasure and all material prosperity. This is the regular routine of life, and those who do not wish to follow it are looked upon as crazy people. Thus all are trained from childhood, but are they helped by this method of education? No! It makes them weak and dependent, because it binds them to the material plane. True morality will come only when we depend on our true Self. You wish to make your children moral, but to do this you must hold up before them the right ideal which will give them real strength. Do not give them the weakening thought that they must depend on material things for their happiness, but tell them, from their childhood, that they are Spirit, and not the physical body; that they are the Immortal Self, which is above all external conditions. Only thus will you make them strong and great powers. No weak person can realize the Supreme Self. At present we think ourselves weak, and we have become so, but let us cease to think it, and all weakness will drop off. Do not remind any one of his weakness. Make even a criminal feel the best that is in him.

If you wish to help any one, do not regard his weak side, but call out all that he has of good; only so will you help him to realize his better nature. However hard it may be, we must all seek realization, for in that alone shall we find real peace.

There are three different paths we may take to attain this end, but all lead to the same goal, Supreme Realization. One who merely works for the Self gets this realization, another who has faith in the Lord—the same Lord whom the worker worships in another form—also realizes Him; while the *Jnâni* who travels by the path of "*neti, neti*" (not this, not this) also reaches Him. As when you enter a dark room, to get some article, you pass from one object to another, saying "Not this," until you find the thing you want; then you cease your search; so also the *Jnâni* puts aside one worldly object after another until he finds that for which he was searching, and so attains the goal. Thus the first class—the workers—by entire unselfishness, giving all their labor freely and without a thought of personal gain, make every deed an act of worship, are purified in heart and attain realization. The second class—the *Bhaktas,* or devotees—worship the Lord with intense single-hearted devotion, and through that reach union with the Divine Object of their worship and attain realization. The last-mentioned class—the *Jnânis*—take the hardest way to reach the goal. Rigid self-control and constant self-denial alone can carry them on the way. Only the strong, mentally and physically, can travel by this road, but he who is determined, and perseveres to the end, arrives at realization of the Self. He sees It dwelling in every living thing, and, thus seeing the Self everywhere and knowing his oneness with It, he cannot hate or injure any being.

This realization is the goal of all mankind. We are all struggling to reach it, though we may not know it. Some have already learned how transitory are the things of the world, and are searching for something more permanent, more real; others still cling to the objects of the senses, but sooner or later all must come to this one goal. "Because this perception of the Self alone cuts all the knots of our hearts, destroys all doubts, and removes all the binding effect of *karma*."

After once having the vision of the

Supreme, we really become blessed; we no longer depend on the outside world, but we dwell within ourselves and become Self-satisfied. The one object of all the religious teachings of the world is to bring unto us this realization; though the path may be hard and difficult to tread on, yet must we march on with real faith and perseverance, and never give up through fear, or discouragement. Forget not the call of the awakened souls who found out the way of immortal bliss, but "Arise! awake, and stop not till the goal is reached!"

VI

SELECTIONS FROM UPANISHADS

AND

OTHER SCRIPTURES

DISCRIMINATION

"The good is one thing, the pleasant another; these two, having different objects, chain a man. It is well with him who clings to the good; he who chooses the pleasant, misses his end."

"The good and the pleasant approach man: the wise goes round about them and distinguishes them. Yea, the wise prefers the good to the pleasant, but the fool chooses the pleasant through greed and avarice."

"Thou, O Nachiketas, after pondering all pleasures that are or seem delightful, hast dismissed them all. Thou hast not gone into the road that leadeth to wealth, in which many men sink."

"Wide apart and leading to different points are these two—ignorance, and what is known as wisdom. I believe Nachiketas to be one who desires knowledge, for even many pleasures did not tear thee away."

"He [the Self] of whom many are not even able to hear, whom many even when they hear of Him do not comprehend; wonderful is a man, when found, who is able to teach Him [the Self]; wonderful is he who comprehends Him, when taught by an able teacher [man of realization]."

—*Katha-Upanishad.*

GOD AND MAN

"Two birds, inseparable friends, cling to the same tree. One of them eats the sweet fruit, the other looks on without eating."

"On the same tree man sits grieving, immersed, bewildered by his own impotence. But when he sees the other Lord [Isa] contented, and knows his glory, then his grief passes away."

"When the Seer sees the brilliant Maker and Lord [of the world] as the Person who has His source in Brahman, then he is wise, and, shaking off good and evil, he reaches the highest oneness, free from passions."

"For He is the Breath shining forth in all beings, and he who understands this becomes truly wise, not a talker only. He revels in the Self, he delights in the Self, and, having performed his works [truthfulness, penance, meditation, etc.], he rests firmly established in Brahman, the best of those who know the Truth."

—*Mundaka-Upanishad.*

REALIZATION

"Nor is that Self to be gained by one who is destitute of strength, or without earnestness, or without right meditation. But if a wise man strives after it by those means [by strength, earnestness, and right meditation], then his Self enters the home of Brahman."

"When they have reached Him [the Self], the sages become satisfied through knowledge; they are conscious of their Self, their passions have passed away, and they are tranquil. The wise, having reached Him, who is omnipresent everywhere, devoted to the Self, enter into Him wholly."

"Having well ascertained the object of the knowledge of the Vedanta, having purified their nature by the Yoga of renunciation, all anchorites, enjoying the highest immortality, become free at the time of the great end [death] in the worlds of Brahmà."

—*Mundaka-Upanishad.*

"The first results of Yoga they call lightness, healthiness, steadiness, a good complexion, an easy pronunciation, a sweet odor, and slight excretions."

"As a metal disk [mirror] tarnished by dust shines bright again after it has been cleaned, so is the one incarnate person satisfied and free from grief after he has seen the real nature of the Self."

"And when, by means of the real nature of his Self, he sees, as by a lamp, the real nature of Brahman, then, having known the Unborn, Eternal God, who is beyond all natures, he is freed from all fetters."

"Let us know that highest, great Lord of lords, the highest Deity of deities, the Master of masters, the highest above, as God, the Lord of the World, the Adorable."

—*Svetâsvatara-Upanishad.*

THE "DHAMMAPADA"; OR, PATH TO VIRTUE

All that we are is the result of what we have thought: it is founded on our thoughts, it is made up of our thoughts. If a man speaks or acts with an evil thought, pain follows him, as the wheel follows the foot of the ox that draws the carriage.

All that we are is the result of what we have thought: it is founded on our thoughts, it is made up of our thoughts. If a man speaks or acts with a pure thought, happiness follows him like a shadow that never leaves him.

The virtuous delights in this world,

and he delights in the next; he delights in both. He delights and rejoices when he sees the purity of his own work.

Earnestness is the path of immortality, thoughtlessness the path of death. Those who are in earnest do not die; those who are thoughtless are as if dead already.

Having understood this clearly, those who are advanced in earnestness delight in earnestness, and rejoice in knowledge of the elect.

If an earnest person has roused himself, if he is not forgetful, if his deeds are pure, if he acts with consideration, if he restrains himself, and lives according to law—then his glory will increase.

By rousing himself, by earnestness, by restraint and control, the wise man may make for himself an island which no flood can overwhelm.

These wise people, meditative, steady, always possessed of strong powers, attain to Nirvana, the highest happiness.

If you see a man who shows you what is to be avoided, who administers reproofs, and is intelligent, follow that wise man as you would one who tells of hidden treasures; it will be better, not worse, for him who follows him.

Do not have evil-doers for friends, do not have low people for friends: have virtuous people for friends, have for friends the best of men.

Few are there among men who arrive at the other shore; the other people here run up and down the shore. But those who, when the law has been well preached to them, follow the law, will pass over the dominion of death, however difficult to cross.

There is no suffering for him who has finished his journey, and abandoned grief, who has freed himself on all sides, and thrown off all fetters.

The gods even envy him whose senses, like horses well broken in by the driver, have been subdued, who is free from pride, and free from appetites; his thought is quiet; quiet are his word and deed, when he has obtained freedom by true knowledge, when he has thus become a quiet man.

If a man holds himself dear, let him watch himself carefully; during one at least out of the three watches a wise man should be watchful.

Let each man direct himself first to what is proper, then let him teach others; thus a wise man will not suffer.

If a man makes himself as he teaches others to be, then, being himself well subdued, he may subdue others; for one's own self is difficult to subdue.

He who gives himself to vanity, and does not give himself to meditation, forgetting the real aim of life and grasping at pleasure, will in time envy him who has exerted himself in meditation.

Let a man leave anger, let him forsake pride, let him overcome all bondage! No sufferings befall the man who is not attached to name and form, and who calls nothing his own.

He who holds back rising anger like a rolling chariot, him I call a real driver; other people are but holding the reins.

A man is not learned because he

talks much; he who is patient, free from hatred and fear, he is called learned.

A man is not a supporter of the law because he talks much; even if a man has learnt little, but sees the law bodily, he is a supporter of the law, a man who never neglects the law.

A man is not an elder because his head is gray; his age may be ripe, but he is called "Old-in-vain."

He in whom there is truth, virtue, pity, restraint, moderation, he who is free from impurity and is wise, he is called an elder.

"These sons belong to me, and this wealth belongs to me," with such thoughts a fool is tormented. He himself does not belong to himself; how much less sons and wealth?

The fool who knows his foolishness is wise at least so far; but a fool who thinks himself wise, he is called a fool indeed.

TRANSLATION FROM THE SANSKRIT

BY SWAMI VIVEKANANDA

SHIVO HUM

I AM neither body nor changes of the
 body;
Nor am I senses or object of the
 senses.
I am Existence Absolute, Knowledge
 Absolute, Bliss Absolute;
 I am He, I am He.
 (Shivo Hum, Shivo Hum.)

I am neither sin nor virtue; nor tem-
 ple, nor worship;
Nor pilgrimage, nor books.
I am Existence Absolute, Knowledge
 Absolute, Bliss Absolute;
 I am He, I am He.
 (Shivo Hum, Shivo Hum.)

I have neither death, nor fear of death;
Nor was I ever born, nor had I parents.
I am Existence Absolute, Knowledge
Absolute, Bliss Absolute;
I am He, I am He.
(Shivo Hum, Shivo Hum.)

I am not misery, nor ever had I misery;
I am not enemy, nor had I enemies.
I am Existence Absolute, Knowledge
Absolute, Bliss Absolute;
I am He, I am He.
(Shivo Hum, Shivo Hum.)

I am without form, without limit, beyond space, beyond time;
I am in everything; I am the basis of the universe; everywhere am I.
I am Existence Absolute, Knowledge
Absolute, Bliss Absolute;
I am He, I am He.
(Shivo Hum, Shivo Hum.)

MOHA-MUDGARA

OR

(HAMMER TO DELUSION)

Who is thy wife? Who is thy son?
How curious is this world!
Who art Thou thyself—and whence comest Thou?
Think on the truth of these things, O Brother.
Worship the Lord. Worship the Lord.
Worship the Lord, fool that thou art!

Even from a son comes dread to the rich, is a common proverb.
Take no pride in having riches, or youth, or family-retainers.

Time steals them all away in a moment; full of illusion is all this—
Giving up these, enter into the path of Brahman, and enter into it quickly.
Worship the Lord. Worship the Lord.
Worship the Lord, fool that thou art!

Giving up lust, anger, greed and all attachment,
Think, Brother, who art thou thyself in reality;
One who is devoid of self-knowledge,
He suffers agony in the lightless cell.
Worship the Lord. Worship the Lord.
Worship the Lord, fool that thou art!

In enemy and friend, in son, in relations,
Strive not to make either strife or peace.
But keep an even heart toward all

If thou desirest to attain the stage of
omnipresence in a moment.
Worship the Lord. Worship the Lord.
Worship the Lord, fool that thou art!

Unstable as the drop of water on the
lotus-leaf,
So is this life extremely impermanent.
The company of sages—even for a moment—in this world
Proves a boat in crossing the sea of this
samsâra.
Worship the Lord. Worship the Lord.
Worship the Lord, fool that thou art!

Day and night, evening and morning,
Autumn and spring coming again and
again,
Time playing—life going,
Even then not quenched the hope of the
life-breath.

Worship the Lord. Worship the Lord.
Worship the Lord, fool that thou art!

The body becomes wrinkled, the head
becomes gray,
The mouth becomes toothless, the staff
trembles in hand;
Even then the jar of hope remains un-
broken.
Worship the Lord. Worship the Lord.
Worship the Lord, fool that thou art!

A child engaged in play,
When youth engaged in making love
In old age merged in anxiety—
Not one is engaged in contemplation of
the Supreme Brahman.
Worship the Lord. Worship the Lord.
Worship the Lord, fool that thou art!

As long as there is birth, there is death—
So long is Mother's womb lying (re-birth).
This is the obvious object of this world.
How in this world, O man, can be your happiness?
Worship the Lord. Worship the Lord.
Worship the Lord, fool that thou art!

On! on! and waver not until the Ideal is realized. No rest, friend, 'til that *abode of peace* is found. The heart may sink with despair when even the hardest struggle brings no good result. Yet, that is the point where we most need to show our strength, because that is the test of life. From surface to bottom, religious truths teach but one thing, and that is strength, self-reliance. Let us all pray to the Supreme sincerely and earnestly to open unto us the gate of light, strength and wisdom. May He grant unto the followers of all religions—nay, all living beings—His peace and bliss. Peace! Peace! Peace!